The shopping mall

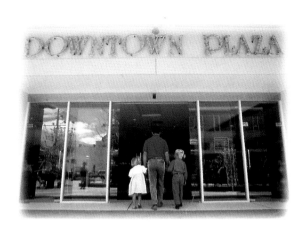

We went
to the shopping mall.

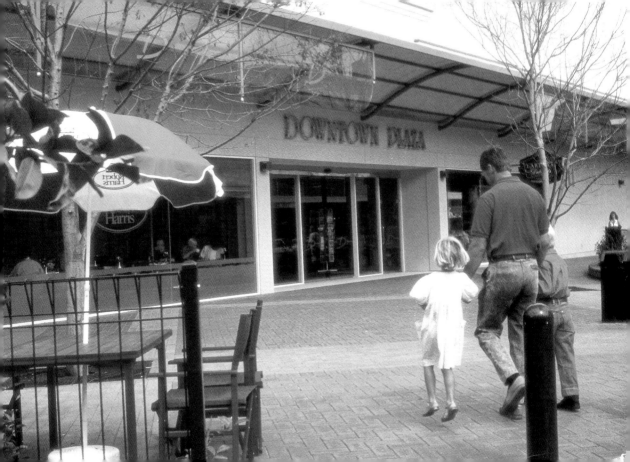

We went

in the doors.

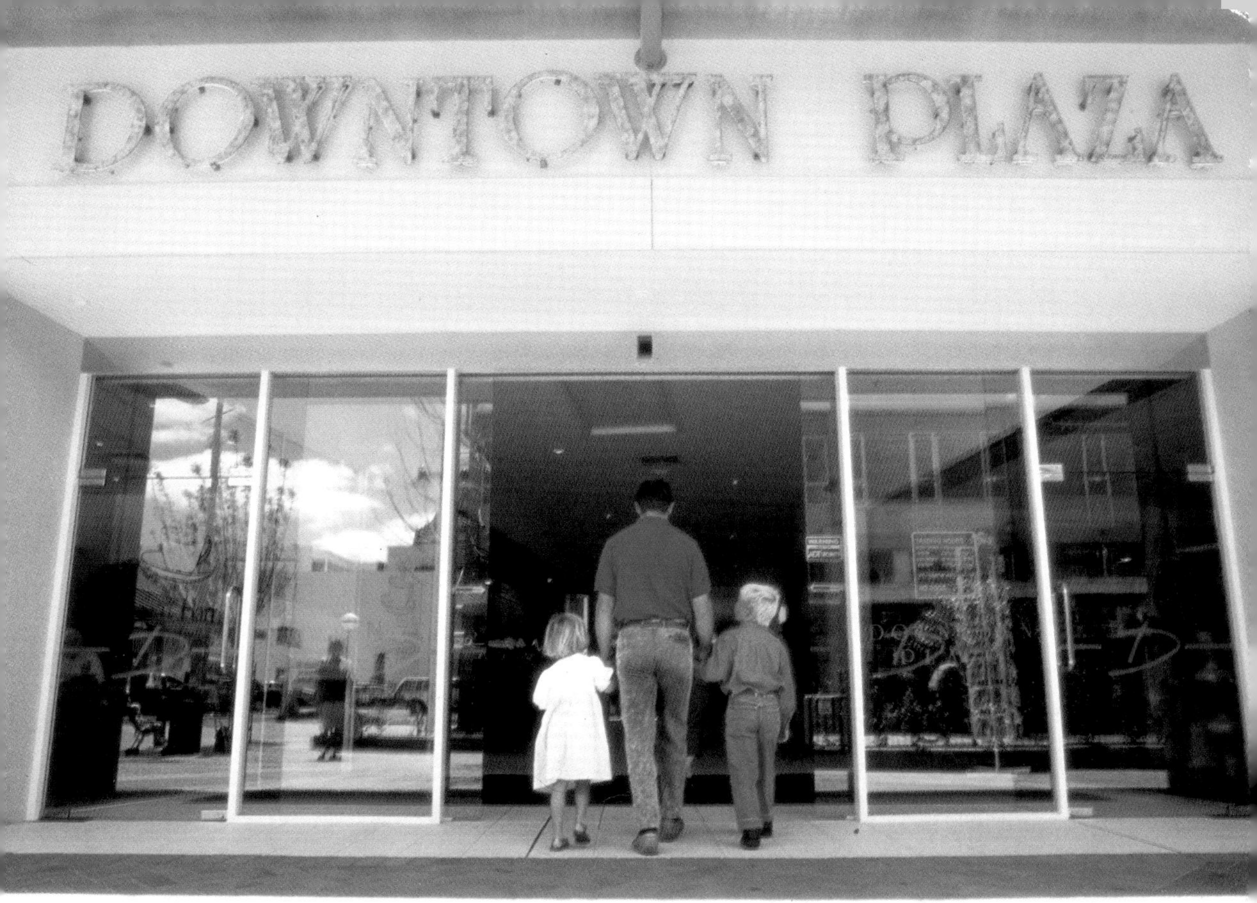
DOWNTOWN PLAZA

We went
in the helicopter.

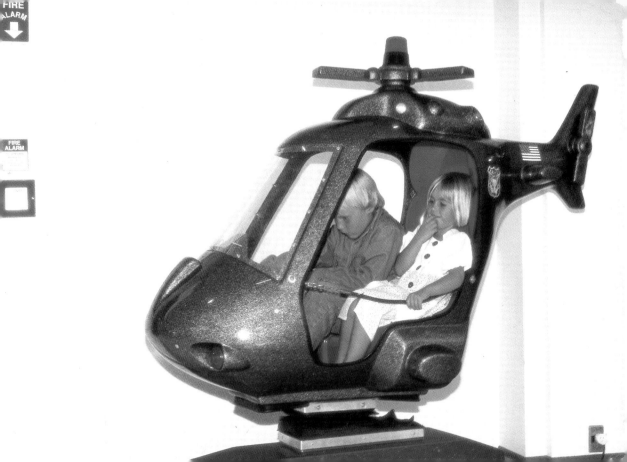

We went
to the book store.

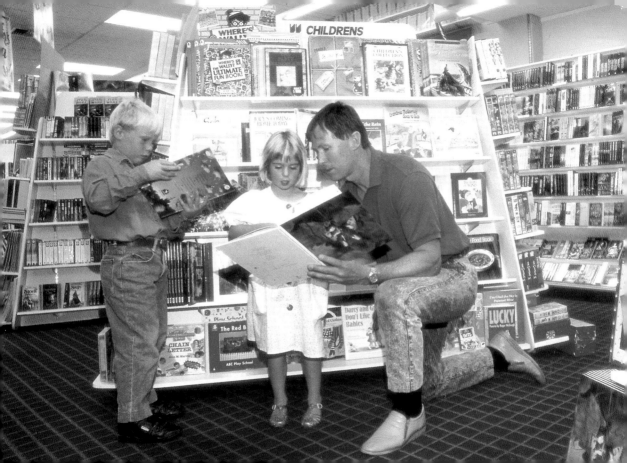

We went
to the shoe store.

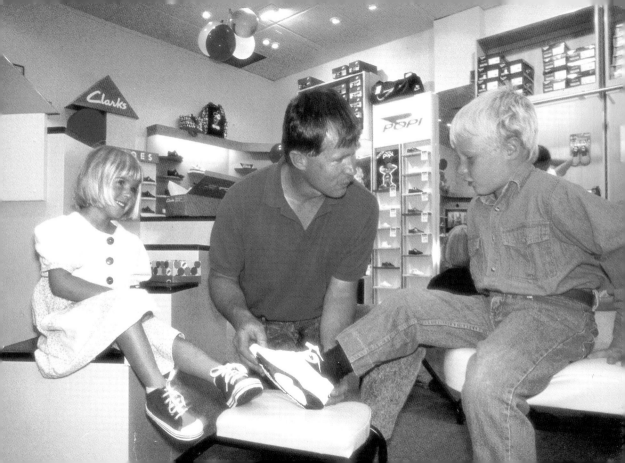

We went
to the toy store.

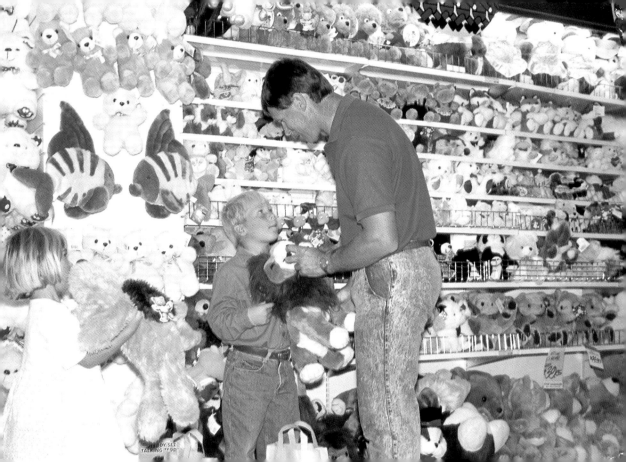

We went
to the ice cream shop.

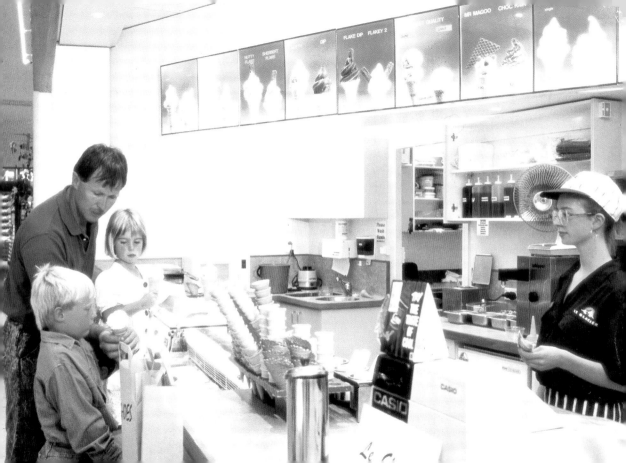

We went home.

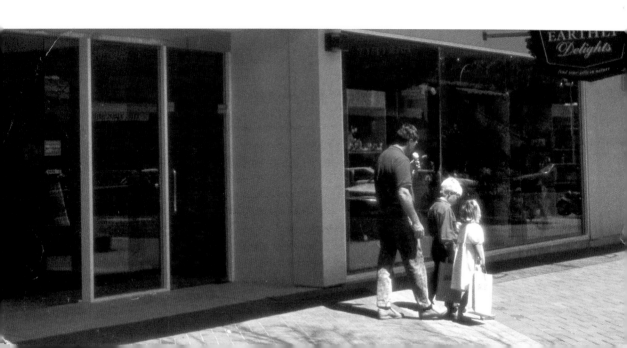